GLANCE

GLA

POEMS

NCE

CHANDA FELDMAN

LOUISIANA STATE UNIVERSITY PRESS
BATON ROUGE

Published by Louisiana State University Press
lsupress.org

LSU Press Paperback Original

Designer: Michelle A. Neustrom
Typefaces: Minion Pro, text; Transat Text, display

Cover illustration: Detail of *Improvisation No. 30 (Cannons)*, 1913, by Vasily Kandinsky.
The Art Institute of Chicago, Arthur Jerome Eddy Memorial Collection.

LIBRARY OF CONGRESS CATALOGING-IN-PUBLICATION DATA

Names: Feldman, Chanda, 1976– author.
Title: Glance : poems / Chanda Feldman.
Other titles: Glance (Compilation)
Description: Baton Rouge : Louisiana State University Press, 2024.
Identifiers: LCCN 2024010706 (print) | LCCN 2024010707 (ebook) | ISBN
    978-0-8071-8247-5 (paperback) | ISBN 978-0-8071-8334-2 (epub) | ISBN
    978-0-8071-8335-9 (pdf)
Subjects: LCGFT: Poetry.
Classification: LCC PS3606.E3857 G53 2024 (print) | LCC PS3606.E3857 (ebook) |
    DDC 811/.6—dc23/eng/20240311
LC record available at https://lccn.loc.gov/2024010706
LC ebook record available at https://lccn.loc.gov/2024010707

for Morri, Noah, and Ella

CONTENTS

I.

Glance

after Richmond Barthé's sculpture Head of a Negro

I.

Then you read the title, which is *Head of a Negro.*
       Child, you think, *a boy,* you see. His cheekbones,

high diagonals, soft with fat, padded, and the eyes
       spaced apart, the remnants of a young, endearing

open-eyed look onto the world. Like a child's,
       the contour-rounded jaw, light cleft in the chin

with the foreshadowing of adulthood there.
       The forehead will lose its smooth plane. The jaw-

line will cut a defined edge you recognize
       in the profile of your own son's face, pre-

adolescent, his brown skin bronze like
       the bronze cast over terracotta. The sculptor left

the eyes hollowed, unfilled, yet they glance
       downward. It's the look of a boy caught

in his own thoughts, how your son looks
       reckoning with his own dialectics. When you look

at the careful left-sided part sculpted in the hair,
       and the curls' lap of brushed waves—you know

someone cares for the child, has taught him to care
       well for himself, the hair brushed so—

II.

You can imagine—your father says,
        afternoon sunlight, hitting the mute button,

in his living room armchair, the TV news hour on,
        the day's overview, which he watches faithfully,

and recounts how lives are broken, breaking,
        videoed, broadcast, by which he means,

the young Black people, who he's angered to see
        captured this way and exposed, and often

dead, in mind if not in body, in brutal circumstances
        for all to view—he says, *who gets to turn away?*

Who's watching themselves dying? Again, and again,
        he warns those closest to him;

he who is more often sunk by what it takes to live
        in this country, to drive down the street, enter a store,

and so now chooses to retreat to what he sees
        through the sliding glass doors:

his bright impatiens in their beds, and apple trees,
        to which he earlier rose on his cane and leaned

until among their snow blossoms alongside the bees,
        surrounded in floral-sweet fragrance,

from where your father says, *And, no one wants you to be*
        bitter. He says that the eyes of this world are closed

to so many of us. He says to you—when you are
      six months into your pregnancy with your not-yet-

born son—*Anywhere else, across the world, your child*
      may grow up, safer, intact, he says, *than here at home.*

II.

Diaspora

You are tracing your origins across continents for a stranger whose eyes draw a map from your features to your children. Hand in hand with the children whose stomping feet leave sand on the marble floor. The café on the Mediterranean Sea, the sea wind billowing through open doors and windows. Your children addressed in one language and you in another. You trace a map of understanding in a stranger's face. The children's fingers dart along the glass case from sweet to sweet. You let your eyes linger on a stranger's face because they hold your face in their eyes. A pleasure. Often enough in your new country you find yourself looked through or around or away from. A vast continent houses both of your ancestors. Your faces tell a story of its opposite coasts. And now. The children receive their wax paper of breaded sweet treats. The loudspeakers play acoustic oud. The stranger tells you his African passage as a childhood memory, and yours, a ship's wake across your face.

The Kinneret

Over the hills in the north, the lake comes into view: azure water.
You see a sea even though you know it's fresh water.

Eucalyptus on the sand beach, fragrant and rustled in the wind.
You dip your toddler's feet in. Kite surfers hover and skim the face of the water.

Picnics, women in hijabs, headscarves, and other women not, divided down the beach.
The children play in the shallows' lip of water.

You see the burgundy curtains tied back with golden tassels:
the mural above the baptismal pool in your childhood church was this water.

The minister lowered a cloth over your eyes and leaned you back.
You arose to tambourines from beneath the water.

You read a plaque establishing the pilgrim's path, which road to follow
to the multitudes of miracles on these waters.

In a new country, you struggle to know what you see and do not see.
To convert is to turn toward another future though the past laps like water.

You learn to read, speak, and pray in another language; some words
come now only in another language as you suspend your weight in the water.

The news reports the daily lake level, at its worst in years.
You drink what's running from the faucet now, the lake's water.

The lake fed by the mountain springs and the Jordan River,
whose borders here shift through time; since antiquity wars over and along the water.

Your child's name means wellspring, a source of abundance.
You hear your child's name in a song: *Come with me to the shore of these waters.*

Ruth

Both of you guests invited for a holiday by a mutual friend. Both of you recent immigrants, recent conversions, both of you the descendants of enslaved ancestors, both of you from the new world. Both of you in your Shabbat white clothes, both of you stand in the living room window, the two geodes sitting on the windowsill, two quartzes, their broken rainbows thrown all over your bodies in the redirected sunlight. Both of you have taken the Hebrew name of Ruth, as your rabbis advised, in honor of the first convert, the progenitor of royal lineages. Both of you recite blessings at the table. You asked her as she asked you what it feels like to leave the people you know. The overlaps like a glimpse in a mirror as you talk about what it can be like alone, when your Ashkenazi husbands aren't accompanying you. Wasn't that part of Ruth's story, too? The new country journeyed to, the newly converted status, but still the lingering questions about foreignness, the one Ruth's husband's next of kin couldn't overcome, regarding her with suspicion.

The Birds Come

everyone repeating you hear the birds are here where which lake pool which forest what wadi what desert rift and when they arrived are always arrived the pre-light darkness in birdcalls the communiqués crossing through your bedroom's open windows the town discordant and dulcet in blasts a Tower of Babel if you need a metaphor to understand living among the courtyard warblers in the Norfolk Island pine in the cedar of Lebanon the laughing doves in the acacia flower confetti the white-spectacled bulbul of Israel your attempts to discern voices among voices kingfishers rasp on the powerline cranes overhead the Syrian woodpecker year-round the Palestine sunbird Nubian nightjar Egyptian goose eagle owl on magnificent flyways across the map's borders if you need a metaphor someone says you will learn to live with such songs at such decibels

They Ran and Flew from You

Your days are ordinary to and from school along the park esplanade.
The children alert as birds and as flitting and as chirping. The sunlight
through the ficus and jacaranda canopy. The children run and fly
from you to perch on the rainbow half shell egg seats. Children alight
above your head onto the mama bird's yellow-ringed neck. A yellow
clump of wildflowers they pull from the ground and suck the stems.
They warn you not to eat the petals, which are poisonous. Into the red
birdhouse, children chatter and *cor-cori-coo* in echoing loops and
in the echo's end, they call out again. You watch them kaleidoscope
like butterflies. They flap and fight over the lavender and spring-yellow
and peach winged seats. You watch the clambering onto the royal-blue
musical instruments emerging from the ground; curling into the body
of sound, into the shape of tuba and trombone bells. The children take off
their socks and shoes to scale a snail's hump. The reward is a tree
dangling its baubles of pitanga cherries—and adjacent a fence's vines
laden with passionfruit—children rip open the top with their teeth and
slurp out the seeds and neon juice. You watch the children assemble a row
before the national flags and the banners sketched with national songs.
You listen as the children pitch their voices in unison.

Shuk

Then in the shuk, in the summer on the stalls' tables, on corner palettes, pyramids of watermelon. Cardboard boxes of rinds. The watermelon the vendor cuts from to offer you a slice as arresting

as the Charles Ethan Porter painting at the Met. The dried tendril from the vine, the gold shafts of light like these falling through the roof's rusted metal sheets. The red-pink seeded flesh, its

unabashed glisten. The dust-green hull under a vendor's resting palm. The yelling out the price over the crowd that your children answer with their hands and dribbled juice down their necks.

What do you find inside you that holds you back? Black, glossed porcelain, wide-lipped, red grin. This import shelved in your chest, as if you could open a cabinet and offer up a pickaninny

figurine gifted you for keeps. You watch the flies and yellow jackets in their delirious zigzags over the pools of runoff from the discards. Arrived and swarming in your thoughts, you want to

find it laughable that you hesitate over whether you can eat watermelon in public as your children grab as much as they're given. You watch them eat, thus far free from discovering

"round, shining eyes, glittering as glass beads, . . . odd and goblin-like." When did you first hear that? When you were young, with your cousins, summers your grandfather carted watermelon

from his fields. The glistening halves he cut on the kitchen table, passing each of you a spoon.

[That was the end of summer]

That was the end of summer   a traveling holiday   a bus

from the center   the air-conditioning you remember   streaming

over your arms   you remember   the sun mid-low sky

orange-sky flare   the torch glow bougainvillea   the bus

driver   the music when it quieted   at the stop   when

the young soldiers approached   halfway   the bus driver watching

you in the rearview mirror   then you knew   the questions

to follow   one young soldier swung the gun around   the other

soldier opened her hand   mutely awaiting   your toddler   so fair-

complected   straddling his fair father's leg across the aisle   briefly

you release your family   briefly   you are a stranger

with identity papers in your hand   the razor wire border fence

blares fuchsia   bougainvillea   briefly you are your own   dark

border   your skin your features   form

a demarcation   an impasse   briefly   an incitement

[The air roiled]

The air roiled with sand ochre sand so that the air was yellow tinged brown tinged orange and the day sunless and the night starless so the heart and the lungs and the eyes in particular at risk in the air the particulates dense and mixed and hovering and swooshing across the streets in waves raising mounds dunes in the streets against building walls in a northerly direction inverted currents and the temperature perilously high the humidity's pulse in the temples people stay indoors and shut the windows and the blinds and inner thoughts drift spiral as the dust soots window sills and lashes the white buildings to stave off the heat the brutalist towers and houses white in the municipalities orange lashed are the cafes the stores close and padlock their gates and the airport grounds flights and the towers slashed orange turn into disappearance across the skyscape the television plots the atmospheric view blotted out land the sand washed air makes life appear barren the days barren locked inside as the outdoors scours tumults pushes us to hide our faces how long will this press down on us reports data mark this swell the worst since the state's founding a wind reversal the wind's long arm vast drag over the region countries wide so inner worries swirl to the warring long standing fractures eroded arid land hostile zones did we they cause the dusts upwell the sand touches residue down on all the built land the trees far crops flowerings leaves sand capped and before the storm wanes every doorstep stained

[Once your family picked clementines]

Once your family picked clementines and kumquats in the winter grove. The air clear and rain rinsed. In the tree rows, the children short enough to run beneath the foliage, to swing around the slim trunks, and tug the citrus into their hands. They will, as they have learned, say a blessing before a citrus wedge hits their lips or the bittersweet kumquat seeps juice between their teeth. They've learned the prayer for each another day they arose with breath. And they lead the after-meal blessing. They've prayed half the year for rain until the winter rains came. Before sleep, their private entreaties append to the Psalms before bed. You watch the sun through the leaves' gloss play light and shadows over your children's faces. When they pray, they mean their voices into the divine. Their careful script on pieces of paper in the cracks of the Western Wall, notes, drawings their God will collect. The winter breeze bites their cheeks and waters their eyes, and they smile. Clementine sweet and chilled in their mouths, which they've sanctified and separated the time without the taste from the tasting, which is what you wanted, the response of prayer from the lips, for when one is not in a grove, not in an orchard, not sure if or how any sweetness may come again.

For the Picnic in the Tel Aviv Art Museum Sculpture Garden

For the picnic in the sculpture garden, the children ask to sit next to the crying boy. Cross-legged, the bronze and fire and jade patina of his skin. The children the same size as the boy. They crouch to try to understand more of his face hidden within the well of his hands. The tears overflow the boy's palms in beads and ribbons, stranding him in his weeping pool. They try to stroke his tensed back, the sides of his feet, to tap his knee. They question: *What made you sad?* and, *Are you okay?* Then, they sit aside the fountain's lip in the sweet grass and eat their sandwiches next to the water's collapse. They stick their hands into the water's edge, and attempt to lean out to catch his tears in their own hands. You sharply warn them against falling in. From further back your children see in the surface's aberrations a reflection of the world around them. Sky and clouds, wavery skyscrapers and gates, and a glint up from the bottom, scattered copper and silver faces. They hadn't seen it before: Why? What are they for? You hand them each a coin. Your child opens her hand to the crying boy and waits. When she accepts that the boy won't move from his sphere of tears, she consoles herself, confesses that sometimes she cries hard and nothing stops it.

Your Days Were Ordinary

your daughter on the walk to school your daughter along her preferred route your daughter with the morning glories how do they behave their velvet midnight-blue faces morning open to the sun faces dropped at dusk your daughter a fine bright summer morning your daughter inquires as to when and how and if your daughter guzzles the honeysuckles your daughter strips papery skin from a eucalyptus your daughter reveals the trunk's cream-beneath your daughter proposes to peel her bark your daughter clutches your arm your daughter queries darker than her preference to grow up to become your daughter hunches to the bee nudged in the red hibiscus your daughter buzzes at the bee your daughter says sorry mommy your daughter says can you shed

In the Gardens, Glasshouses, Arboretums

And when you traveled you visited gardens, glasshouses, arboretums, mazes of rhododendron, rose mazes in the mountains, cacti and snake plants along ochre dirt roads, you stood in the Cambridge Botanic Garden beneath a clone of Newton's apple tree. Left your husband with the child in the stroller and went head deep into prairie grasses, lingered in misted rooms of orchids that had sewn themselves to trunks and limbs, Mediterranean herb gardens on your early morning walk alone you beat your hands through to rouse the aroma—the gardener who crushed the myrtle and rubbed his fingers beneath your nose, Middle East desert oases, a spring where you sunk into the mica-flecked water, naked and hidden among the green-spiked saharonim, espaliered pears on a garden brick wall, the lambs and kids out to English pasture, and the solitude the decapitated monarchy once walked, sycamore lanes along a pond of swans, and sat on the iron bench in Marie Antoinette's secret garden, and stopped the car to wander gravel paths through bees roving in lavender, and boxwood and yew hedge, and the frangipani ringed in red geraniums in the Baháʼí Gardens, the hillside of overgrown stinging nettles you forced yourself through to stay on the wilderness trail, you paid to enter the whimsy of topiary birds and crouching cats, and in your own home, you grew orange begonias in pots against the bedroom window's security bars, because they were easy, reliable bloomers, petite, beautiful faces erupting with no need or expression of a single emotion.

Beach Diptych

I.

The northernmost beach below the rise of chalk cliffs. The tidepools populated. If you were to walk to the top of the cliff or take the cable car your eyes would descend into Lebanon. You have not walked to the top. The children sprawl on the beach shoveling into their buckets. Not so long ago, the war's missiles, the water's warring ships, would have prohibited your leisure. A friend from the nearby kibbutz says as children they climbed onto the roofs of their houses to watch. Like fireworks above the sea. You have read Darwish's account of his apartment tower on the sea, his sudden desire as his building rocked and reverberated from the force, for a proper Turkish coffee. A certain version of the self insists on its orderliness. The next country stays invisible to you behind the cliff.

II.

Recently, so long ago, your holiday at the southernmost beach with friends. There's enough room on the beach for all to have breathing room, you see, an oasis. Seeking yours, you walk through the dunes as far from the parking lot as possible. A feature here you are told are the sycamore figs ancient as Eden. *The eyes of the two of them were opened / and they knew that they were nude. / They sewed fig leaves together. . . .*

You are seeing now. Nut grass, white sage. The sweet water lagoons. You are seeing now the pre-Armistice Arab citrus groves. You see your friend advance with two hands of watermelon for the foot patrol. You see the skewered livers and hearts on the fire's coals. Why only now do you see the netting extended into the sea and the barbed wire fence into the dunes' hinterland? You see the small beach town and Gaza's towers in the background. You see the children lunging into the waves on either side. You see they are close enough to each other to say hello and don't.

A New Year of Trees

Settling the children down at the entrance to the forest, the trail riverside to the sea. The children are giving thanks for the trees. A new year of trees. The guide proposes the children may have some wilderness in their names. Fingers point in the air because they are a lexicon of flora and woodlands. The fir, the rose, the lily. The dove, the date palm, the bee. What do they think their parents wished to bestow on them? The oak leaves' toughness they touch. Peer into the anemone's flushed cup, its beauty known as that of the bride's. If the names tighten tendrils in their chests with the signs and meanings preceding them, they have listened and tracked, but children being children, are wearied of bending down to discern the ground. They scatter wild at the sight of the opening dunes, the promised sea, where the river stops and unlatches its body.

Palinode to a New Year of Trees

But no one and not you amidst the wilderness of those cypresses and rockroses and thorny burnets the inedible mastic and the edible carob. No one called the Israeli common oak here the Palestine oak. The children were steeped in the perfume of white za'atar and wild thyme at their feet. Olive tree branches thick and convoluted. No one and not you put a question to what went unseen. The wind, the differential air, shirred the leaves with nothing explicit. The grasshoppers clicked and arced away ahead of their steps. No one told the children on the soft-bedded floor of Aleppo pine needles. Their moment of fullest attention to their surroundings. Distinguishing the characteristics of those cormorants in the eucalyptus. Even though the children attuned and open to quiver and agitation in the understory. No one and not you amended those expanses of sunlit arid warmth. Or illuminated the border of histories though the nature signs bloomed flowers in two languages. The tomb of the prophet no one said on the trail was once guarded by a minaret knocked down now or that there were homes left where you settled the children down at the entrance to the forest.

Time for Open Air

A ceasefire and time for open air in the grove. A walk for the children to the macadamia nuts, the sugarcane stalks, the cherimoyas, the ice cream bean fruit, the chocolate pudding fruit. A guard said careful of snakes in the leaves. A knife and sacks in the children's hands for collecting. But a game first for the children indoors long enough. A child wails alarm to start. Then a reversal of their bodies into the low arms of the cinnamon trees. As they master their concealment beneath, a fragrant heat from the branches' rustling rising. And then utter silence and stillness, and then the blank of children.

Independence Day

Also yours, this cadence. This pulse, this pattern. The dark crowd in traditional and Western dress. This steelpan's silver percussive turns your head. The smoke machine disguises the rest of the city. And as if the city forgot this audience. Another year. The mainstage elsewhere and this dark crowd's off-site event. The sparklers' frantic spurts in children's hands. Tonight, your faces' dark sparks among faces dark. The strobe lights' beam and break. You see the backdrop's radiating Pan-African red black green. The Lion of Judah. The fist. The African continent drawn across chests. This conglomeration of Hebrew, Amharic, and English. When the local MC inflects a disaffection for these date palm–lined streets, the kiryat towers the police cruise, the dark refugees' tents in the sands next to the sportsplex. The crowd's recognition humming *nah nah* into a nigun. The aftermath of another year. A song sung as a ner neshama, flame of each lost dark youth's name. The kirar interlude. Dark children hoisted on parents' shoulders; small flags frenzied in their small fists. This call you hear; this singing a beseech in Psalm, a call for Zion.

[Any given day]

Any given day you find your child upside down on the rope ladder in the mango tree. Your other child in the garden planting lemongrass starts. No one wants to go home from day care quite yet. The children scatter—as the parents arrive through the gate—back to their play. Today, it's a canal they're building. Today, they've made it turn a bend and deepened its channel. Each day you ride out the last minutes of their stalling with the teachers. Each day a few details to know what the children have done and said and seen. You talk to the teacher your child loves most by the white-washed wall where the children draw with charcoals an evolving world of geometries, waves and parabolic storms over and through their stick figures and houses and gardens. The teacher and you talk in your new tongue. She asks you slowly, in the simplest terms, what you understand of the latest protests in the city: Us, Black and brown, in the Tel Aviv streets, and the police with tasers and tear gas. For now, the children are worlds away, busy hoisting buckets of water together from the outdoor sink. Their stick and jute boats wait on the bottom of the dry canal. Will you admit part of your own heart's plunge? an unspoken hope to extend childhood by leaving your home country for this one? The family asked the protesters to wait while they sat shiva and mourned the police killing their unarmed son. They can only wait so long. The children scream for your attention to their creation. You turn with the parents and teachers to watch the outcome.

Mosaic

You look under the low tent sheltering from the sun, the compromise in showing them, the best way to protect the color is to keep them covered, as if under the surface of the dry, sandy dirt as they were before excavation. The pigmented stones, none of them larger than a tooth, and the picture coming into view, someone's home almost two thousand years ago. This mosaic a floor, a main entryway to receive visitors and to impress with the decorative edge's finish, a twisting helix of infinity. At the corners, boars mid-leap in pursuit of grapes. The deer in the center who've looked up, their sudden alarm, the twin strain of their necks. What about their alertness puts you on guard, reminds you how appearances can darken a threshold? The reassembly of how you see, are seen, in each new country when traveling. Was that a body's shifting stance? What was whispered upon entering? Was that curiosity or a gaze hardening?

The Dead Sea

that day the sea   looked like a mirage   the sky's inversion
in water   as if in a time   where the world's turned

blue vertigo   a last-minute trip   you've brought your children
along with friends   if you put a name to that blue   the water sky close

to the haint blue   your grandmother painted   the doorway
to ward off   or your friends who say   the pure cyan

of the evil eye   keinehora   the tongue of their parents   as in
keep us safe from cruelty's gazes   the shore's encrusted, crested

the children love their bodies levitating   even if burning
in the salt   the white and tan cliffs   the deep descent until

you are as low as possible   negative sea level   waves of heat
across the distance   until it trembles with rips tears   to the very air

of the day   as you see Lot's wife   or the reminder of her
the Mount Sodom   worn salt column   how difficult it would be

even with divine warning   to not turn back   to not check if
even grown daughters   escaped   could you bear to not look

at the city in flames   and how could you continue   leaving
them to die?   Your thoughts suspend   stunned   the sunlight

blinding at every turn   the salt's bitterness on your lips

[You alter the path once]

You alter the path once and when the children see the shadows in the alcove under the school's front steps, the bars, the downy white plumage, the herb-green feathering, you walk closer to peer into the aviary at the parrots and parakeets. "Hello," you said, and the birds said nothing. "Hello," the children said in their language. The eyes and heads swivel and tilt, speaking back; their conversation continuing beyond your vocabulary. The last school bell rings. The keeper dousing the floor and scrubbing. The food bucket's chunks of pumpkin, pomegranate, and broccoli. The children's delight as the parrots are fed what they request. This solidified the new route in your child's head, a map of the way home. Your child's new school, past the birds, past the after-school rush on the snack kiosk, Cyrillic licorice and chocolate candies you'd once bought to memorize the wrappers of each taste. The last landmark, the children's library, one corner from home. Your child permitted to check out books, reads to you before bed in the language he speaks with everyone except you. It's your child's patience, his quick translations and corrections, that allow you to understand the story.

III.

First Winter

Where should I have been? In college,
my first winter, the afternoons I took
the underground tunnels toward the halls

and turned instead for the basement
bookstore or the theological seminary—
its walls lined with stones from ancient civilizations,

a cuneiform from the Arabian Sea, a block from
a Jaffa minaret, a script chiseled in Greek.
It was the time of year you could freeze

outside; exposed to cold, the skin was frostbit
in minutes. Underground, the pipes overhead
hissed as I took the stairs up to the chapel.

In the sanctuary, I repeated a childhood prayer
I knew some of the words to. I'd skip
a lecture and want to skip them all—

away from home for the first time, grotesques
marked the gates at the campus entrances,
I breathed the must of old buildings,

I walked around with a cloistered feeling
in my chest. I could see from my residence hall
Lake Michigan, crystalline by degrees,

until ice overtook it completely.

The Age of Discovery

Again, I hear my father as when he beheld my adolescent face, his measured, factual tone, as if what he saw would take time to excise. I often felt I was viewed as something to be quarried, my face like unworked stone, for how often he cut in mid-conversation, mid-meal, mid-afternoon: *Contrary to your surroundings,* or *Don't be fooled, more of the world than not is Black and brown like you*—I stand in the museum, stare at the tapestries, the Age of Discovery paintings, the hunters gallantly dressed, the women at rest in the grass, the drama of the chase, a dog's teeth-bared grip onto a hind leg, and when there at all, in the background, a coat draped over the arm or reins in the waiting hands of a Black subject.

Who Plays . . .

after the painting Past Times, *by Kerry James Marshall*

But what of the bluebirds in the painting's grand landscape bannering the air, *Who plays . . . all of heart and . . . skill / Will also work with heart and will,* over the Black folk in their leisure whites, day-boating on the lake, setting the weekend picnic on the lawn? The bluebirds' sweet technicolor wings and breasts in a Disney true blue, their industrious beaks swoop along the unwavering sign. You could complete this message in the banner's folds, as if written on your doorpost and on your forehead, strained in the voices of your mother and father, their treatises on excellence, on the couches of your aunts and uncles, striping your childhood deaconesses' peppermints. The Girl Scout troop leaders' badges in your eager open hand. Your hairdresser a doctor of philosophy, a professionally trained operatic soprano, who straightened hair on the weekends in her basement, the Black professional women wrapped in the beauty of this song. In the Black school teachers' rooms your parents requested. In the supermarket line, your mother and the Black clerk alley-ooped a rapture of progress. The bluebirds bear the presence of what was served like sermon at dinner, tucked in your nighttime prayers, pressed among your clothes when your parents said let's go for a Sunday drive amidst the tree-lined streets, even if that white neighborhood raised its eyebrows and bulged its eyes. The words laced the radio, darted in the sun splotches along the car windows, ribboned your braids, each note a thin whistle through your teeth as you stared back in a state of repose at anyone's stares. The winged message escorting your family's move out to the suburbs. When you closed your eyes in that new house, there you reclined in your new childhood bed. The room's pattern on the curtains, duvet, and wallpaper you chose, the repeating motif of climbing thorny roses.

Roses—Fancy Still Life, Still Life with Roses

after the painting by Robert S. Duncanson

You see Duncanson's roses, white and yellow roses, unblemished leaves, individuated, not delicate, not a soft touch in their moment of strongest bloom, or about to bloom, caught in their process of revelation and will to form a blazoned spray. The painter has thickened the petals to substantiality with visible strokes, dabs of impasto. *Full, double bloom, dark button eye,* and *urn.* What do they see? What do they hold? You are hoping for a message in these representatives of the antique, heritage, historic rose from a free painter of color painting roses pre–Civil War.

A white tinged with bone and a yellow hinting a darkened gold. Are they the Victorian floriography of death and greed? Or, the white and yellow emissaries of new beginnings, hope, peace. You can see there's a declarative atmosphere. A mass of flowers, un-vased, lay on their sides, clipped stems in the air. Is there a statement in the depth of contrast from the shadowed green-black foliage to the petals in painterly light? At the least their heft must have pressed thorns into the chest. Their perfect hardiness, like an old master precision, technical ardor, a kind of armor.

In Aaron Douglas's Murals at Fisk University

the narrative winds forward and back   a shackled man's gaze already meets
the North Star before he boards a slave ship   the celestial spin set

in motion   a figure peering in a microscope lens   angles   bends
in plantation fields   colossal arches and skyscrapers   When my parents

first brought me to the library   I turned in circles   to view
the panorama   The light painted like prophecy   its descent and ascent

a sweeping radius   the lance of its slants like an anointing
a bundle balanced on a head   like an Atlas   high above the library tables

the golden oak bookshelves   the bent, studying heads   lest they forget
the realms riding on their shoulders   those who came before

what they've conveyed   and later   my father's hand hammering
down on the dinner table   his ironclad will   his lecture

you must be somebody   the scaffolding built   with each breath

Because My Father Spent a Great Portion of His Working Life Traveling

in the attic now, the loaded slide carousels in their Kodak boxes. I've seen my father all over the globe, through his lens, in his voice. It's his narration I hear when I enter the Louvre's Rembrandt room. His winter day virtually alone with the self-portraits thirty years ago. My father enraptured by the younger Rembrandt's velvet nap, the gold braid along his cap, the flash of a gold earring. Eyes full of his own ambitions, and his haughtiness and cultivation in the next. And to portray as equally, one of the final self-portraits, his last finery, his face's lost tone, mottled. Rembrandt's illumination exposing each furrow, each widened pore, the broken capillaries crazing his nose and cheekbones. My father sees that I've seen him all along, the diary of his body, its places of eye-opening pleasure, the pictures that trap him now as he once was, among the world's treasures.

Man in Tidal Blue

after the pigment print by Derrick Adams

There was the draft. There was the war overseas. There was the domestic base
where I was stationed. My education was saving me. There was my work
in the military laboratory. I wore fatigues beneath my lab coat. The substrates'
and reagents' names were hidden from me in a code string. I had one repeating
function in the experiment's chain. There were relaxed regulations at our post.
Some officers dispensed with our salutes. Our hair grew out. There was open dissent
among the officers at the off-base bar. There was *bullshit war.* There was a theater.
There were long walks along a lakeside beach. I felt free to say I felt America
changing insomuch as I joked around with white boys. There was mutual laughing.
Mock preparations to keep us in shape. There was a sense we escaped the worst
fates. I was beginning to look forward to the future, like it belonged to me
as certainly as the blue air.

Money Tree

after the sepia-print photograph by David Hammons

A shine to the bark, silver leaves aflicker
and the wound that made the basketball hoop:
a bicycle's metal wheel gouged in the tree,
the trunk's burred lip that clamps it.

Whose childhood monument is this?
In the foreground of whose childhood home,
its blind-drawn windows? Where is the adolescent
of the grass and weeds, after school? The adolescent

of the fluid leap and jump shot? Of the glissando
stride and lay-up? The plosive *woop woop* cries sent up
when the body satisfies the calculating eye?
O tree ashimmer in hypotheticals' blooms—

where's the undissuaded youth who sought
a scarce grace here? Who sought to make bank?
The shoulder and arm and wrist on repeat
even as day went thoroughly dark

who refused to come inside until they exhausted
the audience of their mind? *O* extraordinary dunk,
O hard slam, shudder the immovable tree.
Where is the glimmer of a sign

one might one day rise among the ordinals
to be ranked *first, first, first?* Wouldn't
it be possible? Because *if not, if not, if not.*

As a Side Note to a Side Note in the History

Appearing as a side note to a side note in the history. A grave in the old Presbyterian cemetery. A surname from the early eighteenth century, distinctive enough you can follow the lineage back across the South to the "vinegar color skies" of southeast Ireland. In a side note you can follow the lineage to an

"ardent Whig," a "brogue quite rich . . .," a "genial . . ." man who "conceived an idea" and appears riding a horse, outwitting Tories in a South Carolina forest, which distinguishes him as the hero in a side note to the American Revolution. A side note you can follow to a begotten son, a legislator-Nullifier-slaveholder. Also in

a grave in the old Presbyterian cemetery. It's probably him, or next of kin, or once, twice removed, in this early American South district, distinguished by its nickname *Little Ireland,* that my mother found in her DNA along with the darkened swath across Central and West Africa. It's from this corpulent

chunk of Scotch-Irish, vinegar-shaded on the DNA analysis world map, that my mother's mother's father's father's surname derives, born on the plantation of the distinctively named legislator-Nullifier-slaveholder as one of the legislator-Nullifier-slaveholder's enslaved persons. Many of the descendants

of enslaved descendants with the distinctive name have mapped themselves onto a digital genealogy page to follow the lineage. More accurately, the family tree is behind a paywall screen with strings of identity-protective codes, which when clicked open other windows of identity-protective codes, and

so on and so forth, all connected to the distinctive name of the legislator-Nullifer-slaveholder. Who begat, perhaps it's not quite wrong to say, a unique American opportunity to trace one's family back to one plantation that no longer exists. It is a complete forest under a bullseye of coordinates from a digitized satellite view, one that in all likelihood contains within its vicinity the probably unmarked or poorly marked enslaved's graves, for which the records are nowhere to be found or at least not now existent. And, thusly as a side note in the history, the enslaved with the distinctive name who lived

to see the end of chattel slavery in America such as my mother's mother's father's father, also outlived the legislator-Nullifier-slaveholder, who, according to existent records, did not marry and had no children.

[Toured the imperial medieval castle]

Toured the imperial medieval castle, ate pretzels in the square, another day crepes and black beer. In the Museum für Moderne Kunst was the first time I saw Vija Celmins drawings. Her ocean, crimps and pleats and hard folds in the unreconciled surface. Her night sky, the dark puncturing through to a deeper darkness, the stars mimicking a trueness of stars, her fealty to the billions of luminous points only accentuating the unfathomable—what I thought I wanted art, literature to do, the real world apprehended in the image of the real world. But what then when the real world needs resisting? The language the guide exposes on the tour at a town's turned back, the screaming in the copper and purple beeches, behind a curtain of pine, the Buchenwald concentration camp. The prisoners named it the singing forest.

[Before the children, yours or hers]

Before the children, yours or hers, before serious commitments except this, you flew to see K., your best friend, in rural Germany, you brought with you *The Selected Poems of Rita Dove,* your writing notebooks, your writing pens. Waylaid by the flu, both of you in K.'s bed under the duvet and blankets. You read poems to her. Your eyes traveled the window onto the mid-November fields, a winter crop's sharp green expanse. You sipped a garlic tonic. In your fevered consciousness, you read Dove's poem "Upon Meeting Don L. Lee in a Dream"—her interception and departure mid-sentence from the Black Arts Movement tradition. You both looked up at the train searing through at 300 kmh, the pressure and force of its physics in the air and the ground around you, and once it sliced the green of the farm's fields in two, you couldn't undo the rewritten view.

University Market

I could be found at the University Market and Deli working
from four p.m. to midnight, Tuesdays and Thursdays
after my Czech literature class. My hair pulled back
with a maroon scarf that matched my market polo,
my gold nameplate fastened on. The radio on the news.
The hot dogs' oil under red lights. I glimpsed
myself in a security camera feed on the TV screen,
in a ghosting blued black-and-white. My hands pressuring
a turkey breast into sliced sheets against the blade.
I was learning about the dual worlds of East and West
in Milan Kundera. I imagined my upcoming spring break:
a dark wood Czech pub, biting the end off a sausage
and sipping beer. How I would be far away, walking
Prague's Old Town cobblestone streets in my camel coat,
beret, and mittens; taking the bus to the hilltop spas
at Mariánské Lázně, the curative carbonated springs inside
the fog and tall pines. The buildings' yellow and pink facades
in my travel book, I was saving up each paycheck for it.
The assistant manager always goading me to hurry up,
and too close to me, his hand trailing a seam down
the side of my slacks. I stopped in place behind the deli case—
behind the shelved salads, meats, cheeses, the cooler cases'
frozen treats, ice creams, pizzas, sheet cakes; the boxes
in the aisles I was unpacking and stacking; the cans and
jars I arranged to keep the shelves looking full.
I stopped and saw what I was about to do.

IV.

Our One Parisian Romance

The performance over and the crowd's dispersal into the dark, rain sheened, winter streets. We among them in the amber glow of streetlights, our silhouettes across the cobblestones, elongated and elegant. The restaurant we chose at a late hour, the server's affectionate confidence, leading us with her hand, her *Madame et monsieur, pleased to have a table.* The carnelian ceiling, the slender, vertical mirrors along all the walls, the gilded crystal sconces. The slow, luxurious linger of your hand on my face, our dinner's seductive pace, the long kisses between the courses. Do you remember the mirrors affirmed us infinitely in the room? That relinquishment of caution, wariness: had we ever let it go in America? The side stare, the squint in malice, the black-and-white sting of language, where we learned to stand or walk conservatively apart. Our bodies we guarded then by divorcing them.

[Each of those every few nights]

Each of those every few nights in the first months in our studio apartment, the portable heater warming the kitchen, the windows closed, the curtains closed, the lights dimmed, a little darkness, the street below, the pedestrians' clacking feet on the cobblestones, the cars, the arrondissement, the whole city, our notice of it drowned out now as we turned on the water. The MP3 repeat of ocean waves, their rolling rush and recede, the single sound that may soothe the baby's crying. The drain rack propped on a shelf, the two-burner hot plate unplugged and slid atop the mini fridge, the expanse of the cleared tile counter laid out with the cleanser, lotion, ointment, and drops, the kitchen sink bath plugged. In your hands then, a new body's tangibility. It took both of us, one to cradle the neck and hook the forearm with a thumb, as the other poured the soapy cups. The slippery and fragile grip, the waves' insistent arithmetic.

It Was the Middle of February

In the trilingual synagogue. The seventeenth arrondissement. The building
was unmarked. Its front a reinforced concrete frame, and floor-to-ceiling
one-way plate-glass sheets faced the street. Steel barricade safeguards blocked
parking. The entrance monitored and locked. It was the middle of February.
The lobby table topped with goat cheeses, Comice pears, baklava, bottles of rosé.
A friend of ours danced atop the metal folding chairs and sang. Another
friend ululated. Another friend prayed. I slipped the wine-soaked gauze between
our newborn's lips to drunken him. The double-edged scalpel slash of the bris.
The fluttering howl from the butterfly of infant lungs. We clapped to hear
an acknowledgement of the pain. Then we turned to everyone to announce a name.

Spring Plum

The courtyard plum tree, matte purple-black leaves, the tiny thrust of blush buds, as diminutive as your infant fingernails. The mohel wrapped your foreskin in an envelope as slender as my index finger. We ready to bury it as is the custom. Even in your newness, that flesh served its purpose and can't be kept from the earth. That undergird of chill on the spring wind, the dirt I scrape back with a cracked cobblestone, the smallest husk of skin I prod into the ground at the tree's base. No tradition of prayers to accompany the act, our first concession, the admission of return because as we are, you are, but dust and ashes.

Blue Hour

Our studio's slanted roof windows and French balcony doors, broad panes to the sky. I hold you, as my mother who telephoned on those first days says it's our tradition not to put the baby in anyone else's hands for six weeks. In that time, we blink and stare and blink. And through the hours, I watch the sky's blues become more like bone, nacre, the blue lace of my foremilk, the new-vein blue beneath your skin, a glossed grey-blue fish, my aqua topaz birthstone, the twilight lapis of the mikveh, the midnight navy of my mother's handsewn suit, but the iceberg blue in the soles of your feet, as you colic-cry yourself deplete of oxygen, pitches us over the earth, as if we've angled from our fifth-floor windows over Paris, delivered, untethered above the chimney pots and apartments, severed from the clocks the city is wound around, suspended until your breathing resumes and blushes out the blue.

ACKNOWLEDGMENTS

Grateful acknowledgment is made to the editors of the following publications in which these poems first appeared, sometimes in slightly different versions:

AGNI: "For the Picnic in the Tel Aviv Art Museum Sculpture Garden" and "Shuk"; *Arkansas International:* "University Market"; *Cincinnati Review:* "Mosaic," "Our One Parisian Romance," and "[You alter the path once]"; *Conjunctions* (online): "Glance" and "Your Days Were Ordinary"; *Copper Nickel:* "Time for Open Air"; *Crazyhorse:* "*Man in Tidal Blue*"; *Denver Quarterly:* "[The air roiled]," "The Birds Come," and "Diaspora"; *EPOCH:* "The Age of Discovery," "The Dead Sea," and "As a Side Note to a Side Note in the History"; *Gettysburg Review:* "It Was the Middle of February" and "[That was the end of summer]"; *Harvard Review:* "Blue Hour," "Palinode to a New Year of Trees," and "[Toured the imperial medieval castle]"; *Image:* "First Winter"; *Orion:* "The Kinneret"; *Pleiades:* "[Any given day]" and "A New Year of Trees"; *Poetry:* "*Money Tree*"; *Southern Indiana Review:* "Independence Day" and "*Who Plays . . .*"; *Southern Review:* "They Ran and Flew from You."

"They Ran and Flew from You" also appeared in *Best American Poetry 2021,* edited by Tracy K. Smith and David Lehman (Scribner, 2021).

Thank you to Lynn Powell for her invaluable reading and steadfast encouragement. Thank you to the Gan Shelanu community. Thank you to my family. Thank you to James Long, Ashley Gilly, Michelle Neustrom, James Wilson, and Sunny Rosen at LSU Press. Thank you to Loghaven Artist Residency, Oberlin College, and the Ohio Arts Council for their generous support during the writing of this book.

NOTES

"Glance" discusses Richmond Barthé's sculpture *Head of a Negro*, which is part of the collection of the Allen Memorial Art Museum, Oberlin, OH. The sculpture was cataloged as such when retrieved in 2018 and 2019; however, checking the catalog information in 2021, I found the bust listed as "Shoeshine Boy."

"Shuk" takes its quoted text from *Uncle Tom's Cabin,* by Harriet Beecher Stowe (Henry Altemus Company, 1894).

"For the Picnic in the Tel Aviv Art Museum Sculpture Garden" references the sculpture *Cry Boy Cry,* by Sigalit Landau.

"Beach Diptych" quotes Genesis 3:7 from *The Five Books of Moses: Genesis, Exodus, Leviticus, Numbers, and Deuteronomy* (The Schocken Bible, volume 1), translated by Everett Fox (Schocken, 1995).

"[Any given day]" references violence against Ethiopian-Israelis, including the beating of Demas Fikadey and the killing of Yehuda Biadga, and the killing of Eritrean asylum seeker Habtom Zarhum.

"In Aaron Douglas's Murals at Fisk University" refers to the murals Douglas painted from 1930–1939 in Erastus M. Cravath Library at the historically Black Fisk University in Nashville, TN.

"As a Side Note to a Side Note in the History" takes its quoted text from *Some Heroes of the American Revolution,* by James Davis Bailey (Band & White, printers, 1924).

www.ingramcontent.com/pod-product-compliance
Lightning Source LLC
Chambersburg PA
CBHW032208110725
29471CB00020B/263